CONTENTS

Words in **bold** can be found in the glossary on page 30.

Some of the projects in this book require scissors, a kitchen knife, paint, spray paint, glue, a saucepan over heat and an oven. We would recommend that children are supervised by an adult when using these things.

WELCOME TO THE STONE AND BRONZE AGES

The Stone Age is the earliest period of human history. At this time people made tools and weapons from stone.

PREHISTORIC TIMELINE

MYA = million years ago
YA = years ago

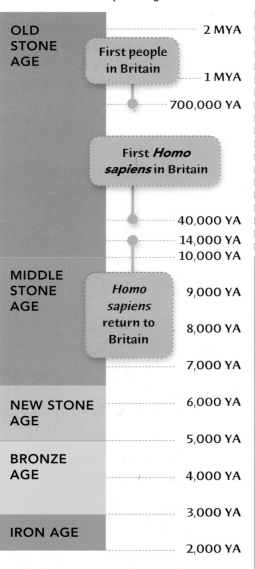

OLD STONE AGE

First people in Britain

- 2 MYA
- 1 MYA
- 700,000 YA

First *Homo sapiens* in Britain

- 40,000 YA
- 14,000 YA
- 10,000 YA

MIDDLE STONE AGE

Homo sapiens return to Britain

- 9,000 YA
- 8,000 YA
- 7,000 YA

NEW STONE AGE

- 6,000 YA
- 5,000 YA

BRONZE AGE

- 4,000 YA
- 3,000 YA

IRON AGE

- 2,000 YA

Today

Prehistoric times

The Stone Age is the longest period of **prehistory**. This is the time before people started to write and leave records. The Stone Age is usually divided into three parts: the Old, Middle and New Stone Age.

When people started to make things out of metal, the Stone Age ended. The first metal used by people was **copper**. Next, people used **bronze** in a time we call the Bronze Age. After the Bronze Age came the Iron Age.

These standing stones on Orkney, Scotland, date from the New Stone Age.

Ice ages

Earth's **climate** changed a lot during the Stone Age. There were several long, cold periods – called **ice ages** – when ice covered much of Europe. During ice ages, sea levels were lower and there was dry land joining Britain to Europe. When the climate warmed up again, the ice melted and sea levels rose. The land between Britain and Europe flooded and Britain became a group of islands. This area of flooded land is what we now call the English Channel.

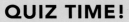

QUIZ TIME!
What did the ice cover during the ice ages?
  a. the whole world
  b. the North Pole and the South Pole
  c. about 30 per cent of the land

Answer on page 32.

Quick FACTS

- The Stone Age is divided into the Old, Middle and New Stone Age.
- People have lived in Britain for over 700,000 years.
- Our ancestors, *Homo sapiens*, first lived in Britain about 40,000 years ago.
- The Bronze Age began when the first people made bronze objects.

Early people

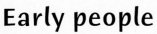

Human life began in Africa and later spread around the world. People first came to Britain around 700,000 years ago. There were several different types of early people. The first to live in Britain were called **Upright humans**. Later, people called **Neanderthals** lived in Britain. Our direct **ancestors**, called *Homo sapiens*, first lived in Britian about 40,000 years ago. During each ice age Britain was too cold for people to live here, so they left. About 14,000 years ago and at the end of the last ice age, *Homo sapiens* returned and stayed.

HUNTING AND GATHERING

Old and Middle Stone Age people did not stay in one place. They moved around, hunting animals and gathering wild foods. These people are called hunter-gatherers.

Mammoths were huge animals that are related to modern elephants.

Big-game hunters

Stone Age people hunted the large animals that roamed Britain and Europe – horses, deer, **boar** and even rhinos and woolly **mammoths**! It took teamwork to kill these strong, fast-moving animals. Hunters probably surrounded animals while they were feeding and attacked from all sides. Old Stone Age hunters were armed with stone axes, clubs and spears. By the Middle Stone Age, bows and arrows had been invented.

How do we know?

Almost everything we know about life in the Stone Age comes from objects, such as tools and weapons. Stone and bone objects have survived while wooden ones have rotted away. Stone Age people also made cave paintings of animals and objects (see pp. 10–13). Experts study these things and make guesses about how people lived.

Stone Age people would have made simple shelters, like this one, from forest materials.

This blade (above) and arrowhead (below) are both made from stone.

Shelter

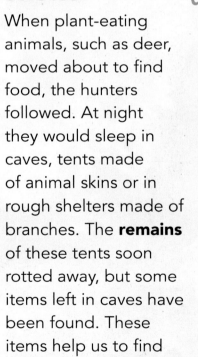

When plant-eating animals, such as deer, moved about to find food, the hunters followed. At night they would sleep in caves, tents made of animal skins or in rough shelters made of branches. The **remains** of these tents soon rotted away, but some items left in caves have been found. These items help us to find out about the past.

QUIZ TIME!

What are experts who study the remains left by early humans called?

a. **archaeologists**
b. **archers**
c. **Arthur**

Answer on page 32.

? What wild foods did people gather? Turn the page to find out.

Wild food

Stone Age people gathered plant foods, such as roots, fruits, seeds and nuts. They collected birds' eggs and honey. They also fished and gathered shellfish from rivers and the coast.

HAVE A GO
Try collecting wild foods, such as blackberries and hazelnuts. Most wild foods are only around at certain times of the year. Keep a log of the foods you gather in each season. Remember to wash any food before you eat it!

Mushrooms

Seeds

Eggs

Nuts

Berries

Fruit

Honey

Beans

Fires and cooking

Stone Age people learned to make fire by striking rocks to make a spark, or by rubbing sticks together. Fires provided heat, safety from animals and a way of cooking meat. It wasn't only the meat that was eaten – every part of the animal was used. Bones and antlers were made into tools and weapons. Skins were used for clothes and shelter. The fat was burned in lamps and **sinews** were used as thread.

Quick FACTS

- In the Old and Middle Stone Ages, people were hunter-gatherers.
- They followed the animals they hunted and lived in temporary camps in caves, simple shelters and tents.
- Stone Age people learned to make fire.

Make this

Old Stone Age hunters made weapons of stone, bone and wood. They chipped stone to make a sharp blade. Then they tied the blade to a wooden handle using animal sinew. You can make your own axe from clay and a stick.

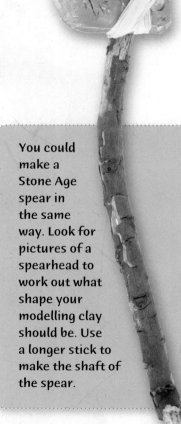

You could make a Stone Age spear in the same way. Look for pictures of a spearhead to work out what shape your modelling clay should be. Use a longer stick to make the shaft of the spear.

1 Cut a rectangle of modelling clay. Shape the edges so it looks like a blade. Make rough marks on the clay with a blunt kitchen knife. Leave to dry.

2 When the clay has completely air-dried, paint it all over with grey paint. Leave to dry.

3 Use a length of raffia to tie the axe head to the stick as shown. The raffia should go diagonally from one side of the stick to the other.

4 Tie another length of raffia diagonally around the axe head and stick from the other side. The raffia should make a cross shape as shown.

AMAZING ART

These prehistoric cave paintings at Lascaux in southwest France, show animals that Stone Age people hunted for food.

Stone Age people were skilled artists. Over 40,000 years ago, artists began to make beautiful paintings and carvings in caves in Europe.

Cave paintings

Most cave paintings show handprints or animals that people hunted, such as bison, horses, deer and rhino. The animals are very lifelike. Some are shown with arrows in their sides. Stone Age people probably believed that painting **prey** would bring them good luck when hunting. No one can be sure what the paintings mean, but we do know they took time, effort and great skill.

Paints

Stone Age artists made paints from **minerals** mixed with water or animal fat. **Soot** left over from fires was used to make black outlines. Coloured earth or rocks were used to make browns, reds and yellows. Crushed chalk made white. The dry, cool, dark conditions inside caves **preserved** the paintings. Any paintings made outside would have washed away.

Soot was used to make these strong, dark outlines.

QUIZ TIME!

Where are the oldest cave paintings in Europe?

a. Italy

b. France

c. Spain

Answer on page 32.

HAVE A GO

Experts think Stone Age artists probably painted with twigs, moss and feathers. They may even have tied tufts of animal fur or hair to a stick to make a prehistoric paintbrush. Try using a feather or a twig dipped in paint to make your own cave painting picture of an animal.

Animal figures

Prehistoric artists also made sculptures and carvings. Animal figures were made from bones, antlers, tusks or clay. Most of these carvings are quite small. Just as with the paintings, prehistoric people may have believed that carving animal figures would bring them success in the hunt.

A mammoth sculpture from Stone Age Germany.

? Did artists carve human figures? Turn the page to find out.

Human figures

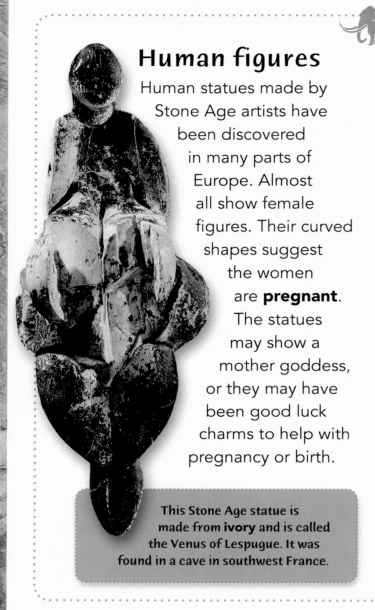

Human statues made by Stone Age artists have been discovered in many parts of Europe. Almost all show female figures. Their curved shapes suggest the women are **pregnant**. The statues may show a mother goddess, or they may have been good luck charms to help with pregnancy or birth.

This Stone Age statue is made from **ivory** and is called the Venus of Lespugue. It was found in a cave in southwest France.

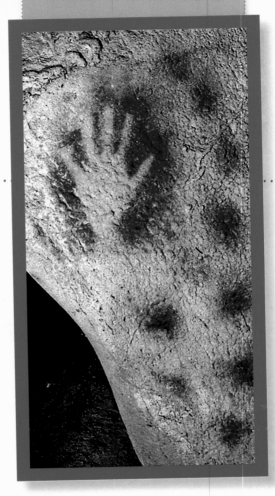

Stone Age artists splattered paint around their hands to make prints, like this one in the Pech Merle cave in France.

Quick FACTS

- Stone Age artists produced beautiful cave paintings.
- They made their own paints and paintbrushes from natural materials.
- Artists also carved animals and made statues of female figures.

Handprints

Many prehistoric caves also contain beautiful handprints. The artist would have placed his or her hand on the cave wall and painted around it. Experts think that both men and women made art like this.

Make this

Make your own version of the Pech Merle handprints to create this colourful picture. Experts think that Stone Age artists may have made them by gently spitting paint at the wall. But you can use a simple paint-flicking technique to create the same effect.

You could use this technique to make wrapping paper, cards or invitations for a Stone Age-themed party.

! Never put paint in your mouth.

1 Dip an old toothbrush into some watered-down paint. Using a blunt kitchen knife, flick the paint over a sheet of paper. Leave to dry.

2 Draw around your hand on a sheet of paper. Cut it out. Lay the cut-out hand on top of your painted paper.

3 Flick more paint onto the picture, covering the hand shape and the background.

4 Carefully peel off the shape. The pale hand shape will show up against the darker background.

5 Keep laying the hand shape onto the picture and flick more paint around it until you have built up lots of layers in different colours. Leave to dry.

TOOLS AND INVENTIONS

Stone Age people had to be good at solving problems. They made many discoveries and inventions that made life easier. The invention of the wheel and metal-working were important steps forward.

Getting an edge

Making stone tools was hard work. Stone Age people made sharp stone blades using a method we call **flint-knapping**. They struck hard rocks called **flints** with bone or another rock. As small flakes of flint broke off, the flint became sharper. This slow and delicate method was used to make axes, knives, spear tips, arrows and other tools.

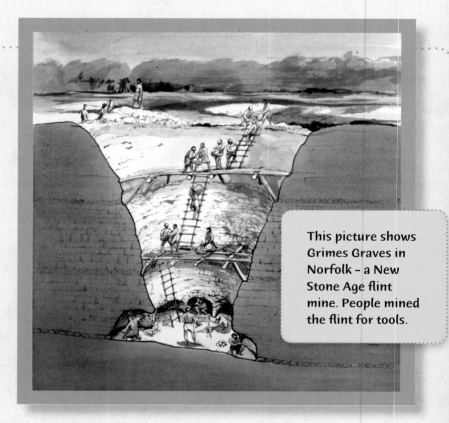

This picture shows Grimes Graves in Norfolk – a New Stone Age flint mine. People mined the flint for tools.

This stone blade has been made using the flint-knapping method.

Into the Bronze Age

Around 4,000 years ago, people started to work metals, such as copper and gold. Rocks containing metal were heated in a **furnace** to get the metal out. Not long after, people learned that adding another metal to copper, called tin, produced a much harder metal – bronze. This could be heated and poured into moulds to make tools, weapons and jewellery. This discovery sparked a new age of technology – the Bronze Age.

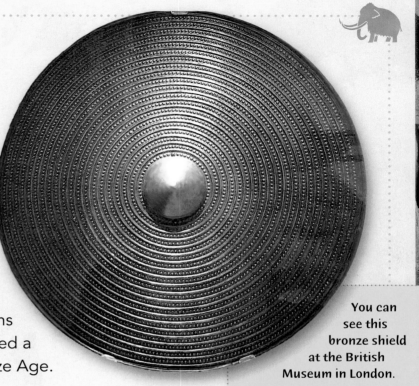

You can see this bronze shield at the British Museum in London.

Mining and trade

Metals such as gold, silver, copper and tin are found in only a few places in Europe. People mined the rocks in their local area that had metals in them and then traded them far and wide. In a time before money, metals were exchanged for other things, such as food, salt, animal **hides**, or finished tools and weapons.

All of these metal objects came from just one Bronze Age site in Switzerland.

? What invention allowed people to make carts and **chariots**? Turn the page to find out.

Invention of the wheel

The wheel was invented in the Middle East about 5,500 years ago, in what is now Iraq. From there, use of the wheel spread to Europe. The invention allowed people to make carts and war chariots. This meant that people, crops and other items could be moved from one place to another more easily. The first wheels were made from solid wood. Later, wheels with **spokes** were made.

Early carts had solid wooden wheels.

This bronze sword from Central Europe is about 3,000 years old.

HAVE A GO

Some of the tools we use today were invented in prehistoric times, but are now made from different materials. For example, Stone Age people used stone hammers; now we use metal-headed hammers. Bronze Age people used bronze blades; now we use steel. Think about modern tools, such as a fishing rod. What materials would prehistoric people have used to make them?

QUIZ TIME!

What is the method used to get metal from rocks called?

a. **smelting**
b. **smelling**
c. **melting**

Answer on page 32.

Make this

Tough, gleaming bronze could be
used to make weapons, such as swords.
The heated bronze was beaten to make the blade's
sharp edge. Have a go at making your own sword from thick card.

The brown paint
underneath the gold
spray paint will give your
sword a bronze effect.

**! Ask an adult to help you cut the
card and use the spray paint.**

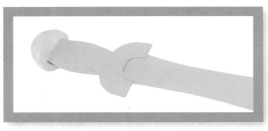

1 Cut out two blade shapes from
thick card or mount board. Glue
them together.

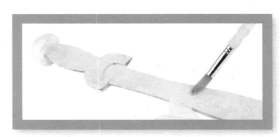

2 Cut out two hilt shapes as shown.
Glue them on either side of the
blade as shown.

3 Cut a slit in half a polystyrene
ball. Push the hilt into the slit.

4 Glue two or three layers of small
pieces of tissue paper over the
whole sword. Leave to dry.

5 Paint the whole sword with
brown paint. Leave to dry.

6 Lightly spray the sword with gold
spray paint. Leave to dry.

THE ARRIVAL OF FARMING

About 6,500 years ago, the people of Britain and northern Europe began to farm the land and keep animals. This breakthrough marked the start of the New Stone Age.

New Stone Age people lived on small farms. They crushed grain to make flour.

Growing crops

Farming began in the Middle East around 12,000 years ago and later spread to Europe. Farmers would save the best seeds from the harvest and sow them the next year. Over time, this led to bigger harvests of crops, such as wheat and barley. The harvested grains were crushed between flat stones to make flour, which was used to make porridge and bread.

Farm work

As farming spread, people cut down trees to make larger fields. New Stone Age and Bronze Age farmers used simple ploughs to break up the soil before sowing seeds. Flint-tipped tools, such as sickles, were used for weeding and harvesting. When use of the wheel spread to Britain, crops were collected in wooden carts pulled by horses or **oxen**.

The flint in this sickle is from the New Stone Age. It was found in the River Thames in London. (The wooden handle is made from a new piece of wood.)

Keeping animals

Around the same time as farming began, people also started to keep animals. In Britain, farmers reared cattle, pigs, goats and sheep for their meat, milk and wool. Tame dogs helped with herding. Families also kept chickens for meat and eggs.

Smaller types of the same animals that we see on modern farms were also kept on Stone Age and Bronze Age farms.

QUIZ TIME!

What are the grindstones used to crush grain called?

a. **queen**

b. **quern**

c. **quick**

Answer on page 32.

? What important breakthough did farming lead to? Turn the page to find out.

The first villages

The arrival of farming meant that people no longer had to move around to hunt and find wild food. Instead they could settle in one place near their fields. People built permanent houses and the first villages grew up. In most places, houses were made of timber, which has long since rotted away. But in some areas, houses were made of stone. A few of these have survived.

At Skara Brae you can visit the remains of houses where Stone Age people once lived.

Skara Brae

The Stone Age village of Skara Brae lies on the Orkney Islands in Scotland. This small village has eight, round, stone houses that were once roofed with turf and whalebone. Built about 5,000 years ago, these are among the oldest surviving homes in Europe.

HAVE A GO
Learn more about Skara Brae by logging onto www.bbc.co.uk/scotland/ learning/primary/skarabrae/ or by visiting it. Find out about other prehistoric villages on the Internet or at your library. Is there a prehistoric site near you that you could visit?

Quick FACTS
- Farming began in Britain about 6,500 years ago as people began to grow crops and keep animals.
- After farming began, people settled in one place and the first villages grew up.

Make this

New Stone Age and Bronze Age farmers used wheeled carts – pulled by horses or oxen – to bring in the harvest. Make this model cart with solid wheels.

Your cart could be part of a display on prehistoric farming. What other objects could you make for your display?

1 Cut out four wheels from foam board. (They should be a bit taller than the cart box.) Paint them brown to look like wood. Leave to dry. Make a hole in the middle of each wheel with a pencil or crayon.

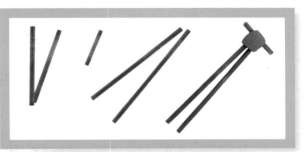

2 Cut two straw lengths, slightly wider than the box. To make the handle, cut two longer straw lengths and a very short one. Paint them brown and leave to dry. Join the two longer and one very short straw with clay as shown. Paint the clay brown and leave to dry.

3 Paint the outside of your cardboard box brown. You can also paint the inside in a different colour if you like. Leave to dry.

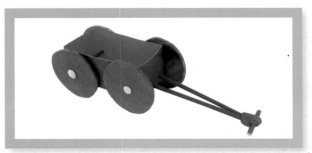

4 Make holes in the sides of your box and push the other two straws through. Put a wheel onto the end of each straw and secure with a blob of clay. Make two holes in the front of your cart and push the handle into them as shown.

THE COMING OF CRAFTS

The New Stone and Bronze Ages saw the birth of crafts, such as weaving, pottery and jewellery-making. Craft objects were traded with local people and people from other lands.

Clothes and weaving

In the Old and Middle Stone Ages, people wore animal skins fastened with bone pins. Later people learned to sew animal skins to make clothes, such as tunics and trousers. At the end of the Stone Age, people learned to spin and weave. Wool and plant fibres were spun into thread, which was dyed using natural colours. The threads were then woven on a simple **loom** to make cloth.

This re-enactment shows how New Stone Age and Bronze Age women used looms made of branches to weave cloth.

HAVE A GO

Stone Age people made dye from bark, leaves and berries. Try making your own dye, using beetroot, redcurrants or blackberries. Ask an adult to help you chop the fruit and place it in a saucepan. Add water and half a cup of salt and heat very gently for about an hour. When it has cooled, use the coloured water to dye a piece of cloth or some wool.

! Always wear rubber gloves when making your own dyes and ask an adult to help you.

Blackberries

Beetroot

Baskets, bags and pots

About 6,500 years ago, people began to make pottery from clay dug from the ground, which they then shaped into pots and baked in a fire. Pots, bags and baskets are very useful objects for storing food and water, or cooking and carrying things. Basket-making was one of the first crafts. Reeds were woven into baskets. People also made pouches from leather or bark.

This pottery drinking bowl, from Stone Age Ireland, was found in a grave.

Ornaments

From objects found in graves we know that both men and women wore necklaces and bracelets. Stone Age people made jewellery from natural objects, including shells, stones, bones and animal claws. Bronze Age metal-workers made gold, copper and bronze jewellery. People also decorated their skin using plant dyes.

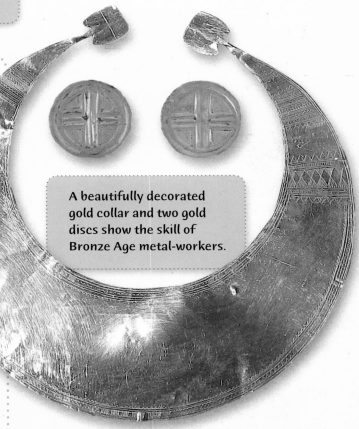

A beautifully decorated gold collar and two gold discs show the skill of Bronze Age metal-workers.

? What amazing find taught us about life in the Stone Age? Turn the page to find out.

The Ice Man

In 1990 the body of a New Stone Age man was discovered in a **glacier** in Austria. The ice had preserved his body and clothes. The remains tell us a lot about how people lived 5,300 years ago.

The Ice Man's body is now in a museum.

The Ice Man was wearing a cloak of woven grass and a leather coat, belt and trousers. He had a leather hat trimmed with fur and leather boots stuffed with grass. He was carrying a copper axe, flint knives and bark pouches containing arrows and a fire-lighting kit.

The body of the Ice Man was found frozen in the ice on these mountains in Austria.

Quick FACTS

- Old and Middle Stone Age people wore animal skins. Later people began to sew animal skins together to make clothes.
- Spinning and weaving began at the end of the Stone Age.
- Stone and Bronze Age crafts included basket-making, weaving and pottery.

QUIZ TIME!

The Ice Man is named after the valley in the Alps, in Austria, where he was found. What is his name?

a. **Friski**
b. **Fatzi**
c. **Ötzi**

Answer on page 32.

Make this

In the Stone and Bronze Ages, people made clay pots to store and cook food. They rolled the clay into long, thin strips and then coiled the strips to form a pot. Try making this coil pot.

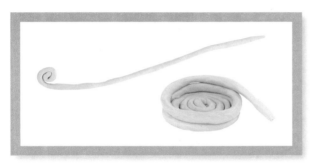

1 Roll clay into long sausage shapes. Coil a sausage of clay to make a flat base. Start to coil more clay sausages on top of the base to make the sides.

2 Continue adding more coils, gradually building up the sides of your pot.

3 Smooth the sides of the pot so there are no gaps or holes. When the clay has dried, paint the inside and outside of your pot.

4 When it is dry, decorate the outside of your pot with spots or another design. Leave to dry.

BURIALS AND HOLY PLACES

Stone and Bronze Age people built some amazing monuments, such as Stonehenge. Monuments and graves provide clues about what ancient people believed.

Tombs

Stone and Bronze Age people took great care with their dead. Some people were buried in stone tombs topped with a huge stone slab. Tombs would often have been covered with earth. Larger graves, called **long barrows**, contained the remains of several generations of a family.

Spirals have been used to decorate this entrance stone to a grave in Ireland.

These stones mark the entrance to a long barrow in West Kennet, England.

Burial customs

Some Stone and Bronze Age graves contain objects, such as tools, weapons and jewellery. This suggests people believed in a life after death. Dead people were buried with things they would need in the **afterlife**, including flint tools, necklaces, animal hides, cups, baskets or bows and arrows.

Several Bronze Age skeletons and objects were found in this grave in Kent, England.

Stone circles

Prehistoric people built stone circles at the end of the New Stone Age and during the Bronze Age. Experts believe these circles were used for religious ceremonies. Priests probably led these ceremonies, which may have marked the passing of the seasons. Stone circles and lines of standing stones are found in many parts of Britain, and northern France.

HAVE A GO
Some of the best stone circles are in Britain. Log onto www.stone-circles.org.uk/stone/ to see a map of all the ancient sites in Britain. Ask your parents if you can visit a site. In France you can visit the famous standing stones at Carnac (see below). Visit www.carnac.monuments-nationaux.fr/en/ to find out more.

Like stone circles, standing stones are important prehistoric monuments. These ones are in Carnac, France.

? What other stone monuments did Stone Age people build? Turn the page to find out.

Wooden ramps were used to place the heavy slabs on top of the upright stones.

Stonehenge

Stonehenge, in England, is one of the world's most famous prehistoric monuments. A **henge** is a circular bank and ditch, which is sometimes topped with upright stones. The bank and ditch at Stonehenge were built over 5,000 years ago. Over the next 1,500 years, rings and lines of stones were added. Some heavy stones were brought from up to 200 kilometres away in Wales and hauled into place. Many experts believe Stonehenge was a temple where ceremonies were held to mark certain times of the year, such as midsummer and midwinter.

QUIZ TIME!

A famous henge called Woodhenge was once topped by...

a. a ring of trees
b. wooden posts
c. wooden houses?

Answer on page 32.

Quick *FACTS*

- Stone and Bronze Age people were sometimes buried with objects, including tools and weapons.
- Stone circles were built in Britain and Europe in the late Stone Age and the Bronze Age.
- Stonehenge was built between about 5,000 and 3,600 years ago.

Make this

Stonehenge took a huge amount of time and effort to build. The large, heavy stones were floated down rivers on rafts or hauled from distant quarries. You can make a much lighter model from salt dough.

Use a picture of Stonehenge to help you arrange your stones on a piece of card that you have painted green. Glue them all into place when your model is complete.

1 Mix about 100g of flour and some salt together. Add enough water, a little at a time, to make a stiff dough.

2 Roll the dough out on a floured board until it is about 1.5 cm thick. Cut lots of short, fat rectangles and some long, thin rectangles with a blunt knife.

! Ask an adult to use the oven.

3 Put them on a baking tray. Ask an adult to bake them in an oven at 180°C for 30 minutes and then put them on a wire rack to cool.

4 Roughly paint the shapes with grey paint to look like stone. Leave to dry.

GLOSSARY

afterlife religious belief that a person's spirit lives on after death

ancestors early humans, or relatives, who died a long time ago

boar a wild pig

bronze a metal made from copper and tin

chariots wheeled carts used in war

climate the usual weather conditions for a place

copper a soft, red-brown metal

flint hard stone used for tools in prehistoric times

flint-knapping a way of chipping flint to make a sharp blade

furnace a very hot oven

glacier a huge ice sheet that moves slowly down a mountain

henge prehistoric monument that includes a circular bank and ditch

hides animal skins that are used to make leather

Homo sapiens early people who are our direct ancestors

hunter-gatherers people who live by hunting and gathering their food

ice ages long, cold periods in Earth's history, when ice covered a lot of the world

ivory a hard, white material found in animal teeth and tusks

long barrows prehistoric family tombs

loom a frame for weaving

mammoths large animals related to modern elephants that have now died out

minerals non-living materials that form rocks

monuments buildings or structures built to honour something or someone

Neanderthals early humans who were not our direct ancestors

oxen cattle

pregnant a woman or female animal who is going to have a baby

prehistory a time before people began to write and leave records. British prehistory ended in 43 CE

preserved something that has been made to last for a long time

prey an animal that is hunted for food

remains things that are left over

sinews rope-like tissues that join muscle to bone

soot a black powder that is made when things are burned in a fire

spokes rods connecting the middle to the edge of a wheel

Upright humans a type of early human, also called *Homo erectus*, who were not our direct ancestors

BOOKS

Britain in the Past: The Bronze Age/The Stone Age by Moira Butterfield (Franklin Watts 2015)

Digging Into History: Solving the Mysteries of Stonehenge by Leon Gray (Franklin Watts 2014)

Explore!: Celts by Sonya Newland (Wayland 2015)

Life in the Stone Age, Bronze Age and Iron Age by Anita Ganeri (Raintree 2014)

Prehistoric Adventures (series) by John Malam (Wayland 2016)

The History Detective Investigates: Stone Age to Iron Age by Clare Hibbert (Wayland 2016)

PLACES TO VISIT

Stone Age and Bronze age art and objects can be seen in many museums, including:

British Museum (London)
National Museum of Wales (Cardiff)
National Museum of Scotland (Edinburgh)

National Museum of Ireland, Archaeology and History (Dublin)
Ulster Museum (Ulster, Northern Ireland)

WEBSITES

BBC website on ancient Britain:
www.bbc.co.uk/history/handsonhistory/ancient-britain.shtml

The British Museum website has information about the Stone Age and the Bronze Age:
www.britishmuseum.org/learning/schools_and_teachers/resources/cultures/prehistoric_britain.aspx

English Heritage Stonehenge game:
www.english-heritage.org.uk/visit/places/stonehenge/school-visits/education-game/

BBC History web page on Stonehenge and Stone Age life:
www.bbc.co.uk/history/ancient/british_prehistory/stonehenge_stoneage.shtml

Stone-circles.org.uk has a map of prehistoric sites in Britain:
www.stone-circles.org.uk/stone/

NOTE TO PARENTS AND TEACHERS:

Every effort has been made by the Publishers to ensure that these websites are suitable for children, that they are of the highest educational value, and that they contain no inappropriate or offensive material. However, because of the nature of the Internet, it is impossible to guarantee that the contents of these sites will not be altered. We strongly advise that Internet access is supervised by a responsible adult.

INDEX

QUIZ ANSWERS

Page 5.   **c** – about 30 per cent of the land.
Page 7.   **a** – archaeologists. They are experts who study objects and remains from the past.
Page 11. **c** – Spain. The paintings in the El Castillo cave are more than 40,000 years old.
Page 16. **a** – smelting.
Page 19. **b** – quern.
Page 24. **c** – Ötzi, named after the Ötzal Valley.
Page 28. **b** – wooden posts.

Franklin Watts
This edition published in 2016 by The Watts Publishing Group

Copyright © The Watts Publishing Group 2015

Series editor: Amy Stephenson
Series designer: Jeni Child
Crafts: Rita Storey
Craft photography: Tudor Photography
Picture researcher: Diana Morris

Picture credits:
AFP/Getty Images: 24t. Alvarezfoto/Dreamstime: front cover c, 1,10-11bg
Amphaiwan/Dreamstime: 22br. Anxela/Dreamstime: 6-7 bg. archaeopark-vogelherd.de: 11br. Artbeat/Dreamstime: 8cl. Asist/Dreamstime: 14b. Darryl Brooks/Dreamstime: 6c. catiamadio/Dreamstime: 18-19 bg. Gaius Cornelius/CC Wikimedia: 15t. Henning Dalhoff/SPL: 5t. De Agostini/Photoshot: 11bl. Designsstock/Dreamstime: 22-23 bg. Dkidpix/Dreamstime: 8c. Mark Eaton/Dreamstime: 20c. Empire331/Dreamstime: 8lb. Andrew Emptage/Dreamstime: 32b. English Heritage/HIP/Alamy: 14t. Richard Griffin/Dreamstime: 19crJune Hawk/istockphoto: 28. Helen Hotson/Dreamstime: 30b. Helen Hotson/Shutterstock: 26-27 bg. Jomaplaon/Dreamstime: 16tl. Mariusz Jurgielewicz/Dreamstime: 7t. Jakub Krechowicz/Dreamstime: 8r. Lepas/Dreamstime: 22bc. Look And Learn: 18c. Robyn Mackenzie/Dreamstime: 8l. Margo555/Dreamstime: 8cb. Marral/istockphoto: 7b. Douglas Mazonowicz/Photoshot: 10t. Richard Melichor/Dreamstime: 26b. Musée des Antiquites Nationales, St Germain-en-Laye/BAL: 16tr. Museum of London: 19tr. National Museum of Ireland: 23t. National Museum of Ireland/Thomas McCaffrey: 23b. Teo Navolli/Shutterstock: 27b. Nevinates/Dreamstime: 8clb. panbazil/Shutterstock: 19cl, 19c, 19bl, 19bc. Arnd Rockser/Dreamstime: 24b. Sandstein/CC Wikimedia: 15b. Sikth/Dreamstime: 14-15 bg. Hans Splinter/Flickr: 22c. Jens Stolt/Dreamstime: 7c. Ferenc Ungar/Dreamstime: 26t. Vivilweb/Dreamstime: 8rb. Wessex Archaeology: 27t. CC Wikimedia: 12r. David Woods/Shutterstock: 4b. World Illustrated/Photoshot: 12l.

Dewey number: 936.0'1
ISBN: 978 1 4451 3746 9

Printed in China.

Franklin Watts
An imprint of
Hachette Children's Group
Part of The Watts Publishing Group
Carmelite House
50 Victoria Embankment
London EC4Y 0DZ

An Hachette UK Company
www.hachette.co.uk

www.franklinwatts.co.uk

DISCOVER THROUGH
CRAFT

THE STONE AGE & BRONZE AGE

By Jen Green

W

FRANKLIN WATTS

LONDON•SYDNEY